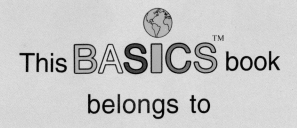

This BASICS™ book

belongs to

....

....

....

USA

The World

The Galaxy

The Universe

First Aladdin Books edition 1992

First published in 1990 by David Bennett Books Limited
94 Victoria Street, St Albans, Herts AL1 3TG, England

Series Editor: Ruth Thomson
Consultant: Martin Weiss, Ph.D., Biology Manager, New York Hall of Science, New York

Aladdin Books
Macmillan Publishing Company
866 Third Avenue
New York, NY 10022

Printed in Hong Kong

1 2 3 4 5 6 7 8 9 10

Library of Congress Cataloging–in–Publication Data
Wood, Tim.
Our Planet Earth / written by Tim Wood: illustrated by Alastair
Graham.
p. cm.—(Aladdin basics)
Includes index.
Summary: Presents basic facts about our planet, discussing
landforms, weather, atmosphere, rivers, and volcanoes.
ISBN 0–689–71589–7
1. Earth—Juvenile literature. [1. Earth] I. Graham,
Alastair, ill. II. Title. III. Series.
QB631.4.W66 1992
550—dc20 91–26681

Our Planet Earth

Written by

Tim Wood

Illustrated by

Alastair Graham

Aladdin Books
Macmillan Publishing Company
New York

Maxwell Macmillan International
New York   Oxford   Singapore   Sydney

There are billions of stars in space.

The closest star to our planet Earth is the Sun.

The Sun is a gigantic, very hot ball of gas.

It gives Earth its light and warmth.

This is our home, the planet Earth.
It's like a huge ball spinning in space.
There are other planets in space, too.
But Earth is special. As far as we know,
it's the only planet with plants,
animals, and people on it.

The distance between the Sun and Earth should really be about 1,182 feet. That is as long as four football fields! We have had to make the distance much shorter so that it will fit on the page.

Earth is covered by a thin,
invisible blanket
called the atmosphere.
It keeps Earth warm and
holds the air we breathe.
The air in the atmosphere
moves around.
Moving air is called wind.

Some of the Sun's rays
are bad for us,
but don't worry—
the atmosphere stops
most of them from
getting through.

There are giant rocks
whizzing through space.
Sometimes, one of them
crashes toward Earth.
But the rocks
are usually burned up
in the atmosphere
before they hit Earth.

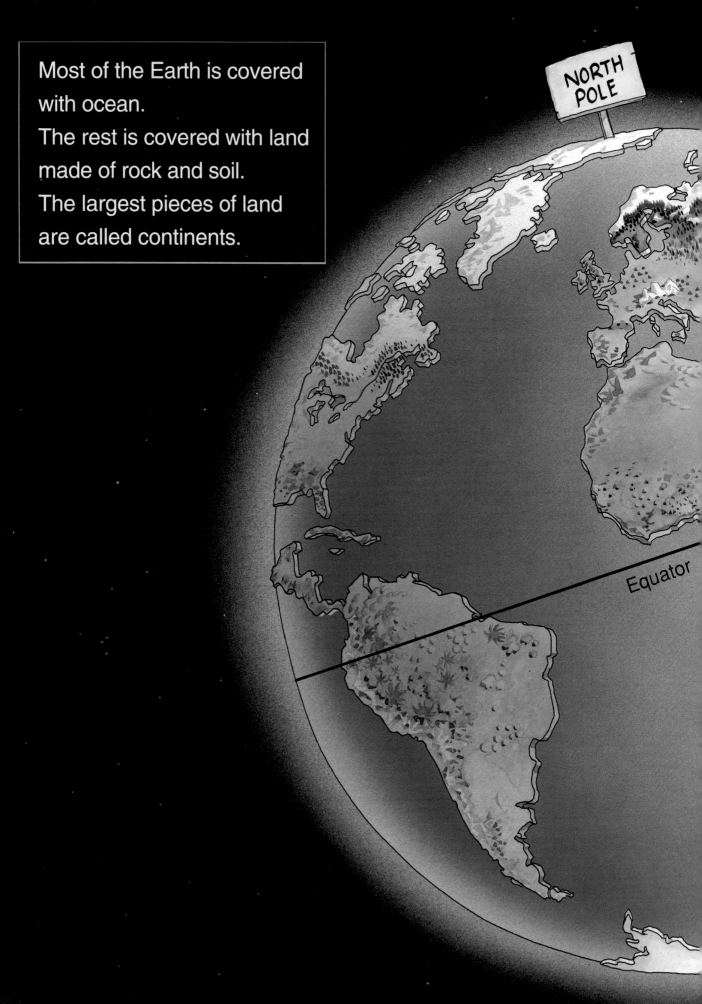

Most of the Earth is covered with ocean.
The rest is covered with land made of rock and soil.
The largest pieces of land are called continents.

The top and bottom of the Earth
are called the poles.
The area around the middle
of the Earth is the equator.
We have marked them
so you can see where they are.

It is always warm at the equator
because it gets a lot of direct heat
from the Sun. But the poles
do not and are always cold.

SOUTH
POLE

The ocean is constantly moving.
Both the wind and Earth spinning slowly
in space cause waves and giant swirls
in the water. These swirls are called currents.

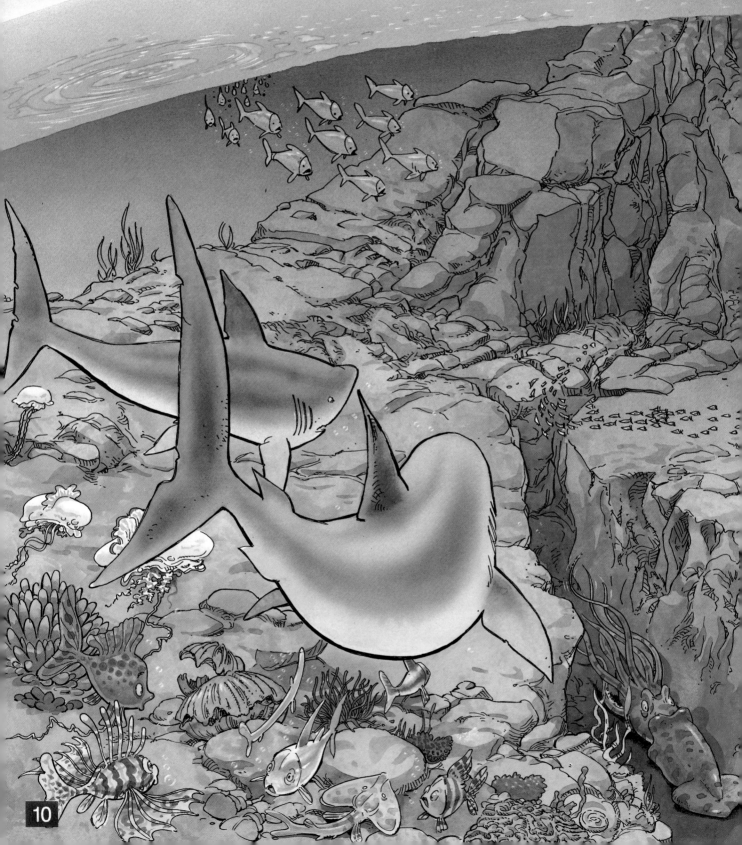

Oceans are not very deep near the land.
But far away from land they can be deeper
than the tallest mountains are tall!
Most of the ocean is full of life. Millions of
different plants and animals live there.

Do you know why the water in the ocean is salty?
People used to believe that it was because rivers
and rainwater washed salt from the rocks
on land into the ocean. Now scientists think
the salt comes from underwater volcanoes.

We live on the thin, cool crust of hard rock
on the outside of the Earth.
But deep inside the Earth it is incredibly hot.
Here the rock has melted into red-hot liquid.

Sometimes this hot, melted rock, called lava,
bursts up from under the ground.
It shoots out to make a volcano.

BOOM!

The volcano explodes!

After a while, the lava stops coming out and cools down. It turns into hard rock.
The volcano is quiet...
until the next explosion.

Did you know that the land moves? Earth's crust is not one single piece. It is made up of several gigantic pieces that float on the melted rock under them.
They move very, very slowly. When two of these huge pieces of crust push against each other, one piece, or sometimes both pieces, are pushed upward.
This is how mountains are formed.

Put a tablecloth on a shiny table.
Put your hands wide apart on the cloth.
Now push them slowly together.
You will see mountains start to form on your tablecloth!

The weather at the top of mountains
is too cold for trees to grow.
When rain and snow fall on mountains,
they wash away the soil.

You will never see some of the highest
mountains on Earth, because they are
under the ocean.

Rivers usually start by bubbling out
of the ground or as a stream flowing
out of a lake. As the water races downhill,
other streams run into it. A stream grows
into a river. A river always follows
the easiest way to the ocean.

As a river flows along, it carries rocks
and sand with it. These wear away
the banks and bottom of the river.
Very slowly, rivers change the shape
of the land. They carve out huge valleys.
Eventually, all rivers flow into the ocean.

The coldest places on Earth
are the North and South Poles.
Ice and snow cover everything.
There is land under the ice at the South Pole.
There is no land under the ice at the North Pole.
Large bits of ice, called icebergs, often break off
from the main sheet of ice and float away.
When they reach warmer places, they melt.

Put an ice cube in a glass of water.
How much of your "iceberg"
is below the water?

Polar seas are very cold, but even they are
full of tiny animals and plants called plankton.
Almost all ocean creatures eat plankton.
If all the plankton in the world's oceans died,
the ocean creatures would die, too.

This hot, sticky place
is a rain forest. Rain forests grow
where the Earth is always hot
and rain falls almost every day.

Lots of animals live in the rain forest. There's plenty of fruit and insects for them to eat. How many different animals can you see in this rain forest?

In some places, the weather changes during the year. These changes happen because Earth is spinning in space.

When the Sun is close to one half of the Earth, it is far away from the other half. One half is warm and the other is cold.

There are four seasons in all.
Winter is cold and snowy.
Spring is warmer, and the trees start to bud.
The summer is hot and green.
Fall is cooler, and the leaves change color
before they drop off the trees.

This is a desert.
During the day, the Sun blazes down
on the rocks and sand.
It's really, really hot.
At night, it gets really cold.

Phew! It makes you feel thirsty just to look at it! The only water for miles around is at this oasis. There's a spring of water here and palm trees that give shade.

Not many plants can grow here, because there is not much water. Those that do grow have very tough skins to hold the water in. Most desert animals have found ways of living without water for long periods of time.

Earth is a wonderful planet.
But some people do not treat it well.
They cut down millions of trees
in the rain forests to clear the land for farming.
If too many trees are chopped down,
the weather in the rain forests will change.
This may change the weather all over the world.

People also dump poisonous waste
into rivers and oceans. Factories
and cars pour smoke and poisonous gases
into the air. Pollution is changing
the atmosphere, and some scientists
are concerned about how hot Earth will get.

If we want to save Earth, we must be more careful.
We must stop changing the atmosphere.
We must plant trees instead of burning them.
We must stop factories and cars from filling the air
with smoke and poison. We must stop
dumping garbage into rivers and oceans.
We must stop wasting metals and fuel.

We must start looking after
our planet Earth.
It's the only one we've got!

INDEX

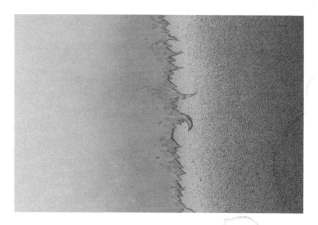
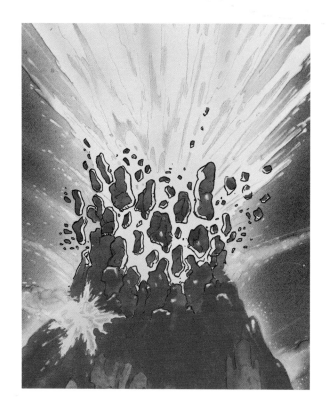

BASICS™

An introduction to our world